African Department

C000068520

Walking a Fine Line

Public Investment Scaling Up and Debt Sustainability in Burkina Faso

Prepared by Malangu Kabedi-Mbuyi, Mame Astou Diouf, and Constant Lonkeng Ngouana

INTERNATIONAL MONETARY FUND

Cataloging-in-Publication Data
Joint Bank-Fund Library

Names: Kabedi-Mbuyi, Malangu. | Astou Diouf, Mame. |Lonkeng Ngouana, Constant. | International Monetary Fund. | International Monetary Fund. African Department.
Title: Walking a Fine Line : Public Investment Scaling Up and Debt Sustainability in Burkina Faso / prepared by Malangu Kabedi-Mbuyi, Mame Astou Diouf, and Constant Lonkeng Ngouana.
Description: Washington, DC : International Monetary Fund, 2016. | Includes bibliographical references. | At head of title: African Department.
Identifiers: ISBN 978-1-49835-853-8 (paper)
Subjects: LCSH: Sub-Saharan Africa—Debt sustainability. | Public Investment—Sub-Saharan Africa. | Economic development—Sub-Saharan Africa.
Classification: LCC HC800.T723 2016

Publication orders may be placed online, by fax, or through the mail:
International Monetary Fund, Publication Services
P.O. Box 92780, Washington, DC 20090, U.S.A.
Tel. (202) 623-7430 Fax: (202) 623-7201
E-mail: publications@imf.org
www.imfbookstore.org
www.elibrary.imf.org

Abstract

This paper analyzes the macroeconomics of scaling up public investment in Burkina Faso under alternative financing options, including through foreign aid and a combination of tax adjustment and borrowing. Our findings are twofold: (1) raising official development assistance in line with the Gleneagles agreement provides scope for financing public investment at low cost and would have positive, but somewhat moderate, effects on aggregate output—the growth dividends in the nontradables sector would be partially offset by the Dutch disease in the tradables sector; and (2) the massive investment scaling-up contemplated under Burkina Faso's "accelerated growth" strategy, while boosting medium- and long-term growth, would lead to unsustainable debt dynamics under a plausible tax adjustment and realistic concessional financing. A more gradual approach to closing Burkina Faso's infrastructure gap is therefore desirable because it would take into account the needed time for the country to address its capacity constraints and to further improve investment efficiency.

JEL Classification Numbers: D50, F41, F43, H54, H63
Keywords: Burkina Faso, fiscal sustainability, foreign aid, growth, public investment
Authors' E-Mail Addresses: MKabedi@imf.org; MDiouf@imf.org; CLonkeng@imf.org

Acknowledgments

This paper draws on two analytical pieces by the authors during their time on the Burkina Faso desk at the IMF. One of them was undertaken to inform policy discussions in the context of an Article IV consultation between the IMF and the Burkinabè authorities (see IMF 2012) and the other was undertaken to guide policy discussions on the macroeconomics of scaling up foreign aid to low-income countries (LICs) to levels compatible with Gleneagles commitments.

The authors would like to thank Michael Atingi Ego, Laure Redifer, Liam O'Sullivan, the Research Advisory Committee of the IMF's African Department (Magnus Saxegaard in particular), the Development Macroeconomics Division of the IMF's Research Department (Felipe Zanna and Salifou Issoufou in particular), and seminar participants in the IMF's African Department for valuable suggestions and support. The usual disclaimer applies.

Contents

I. Introduction

Burkina Faso is a landlocked West African country with an important infrastructure deficit. A World Bank study evaluates the country's infrastructure funding gap at US$165 million per year, equivalent to 4 percent of GDP as of 2007 (see Briceño-Garmendia and Domínguez-Torres 2011).[1] The 2014–15 *Global Competitiveness Report* (Schwab 2014) also identifies inadequate supply of infrastructure as one of the major impediments to doing business in Burkina Faso. Although bridging the infrastructure deficit is important to overcome geographical constraints,[2] funding public investment has been a challenge.

Notwithstanding the abovementioned constraints, in recent years Burkina Faso has been among the top performers in the group of non-resource-rich sub-Saharan African countries (see IMF's *Sub-Saharan Africa Regional Economic Outlook*, October 2013).[3] The buoyant economic activity, while welcomed, put additional strain on already limited infrastructure. Addressing the country's infrastructure gap is therefore critical to maintaining the growth momentum. In this context, the country's accelerated growth strategy envisaged doubling the public investment budget to US$2.2 billion over a five-year period. At the same time, reconciling the necessary financing for the urgent infrastructure needs with debt sustainability is challenging, especially in light of the country's high vulnerability to terms-of-trade shocks.

Against this backdrop, we examine the links between investment financing (including through foreign aid and a combination of tax adjustment and borrowing), growth, and debt sustainability in Burkina Faso. We use two dynamic general equilibrium

---

[1] The study also finds that upgrading the country's infrastructure endowment to that of the region's middle-income countries could boost annual growth by more than 3 percentage points per capita.

[2] The country's vulnerability to disruptions in regional ports was apparent during the political crisis in Côte d'Ivoire, as Burkina Faso strives to find alternative routes for its internationally traded goods.

[3] Gold exports have surged in Burkina Faso since 2011, making the country somewhat resource rich.

(DGE) models that were developed in the IMF and widely applied within the institution.

The first model—"The Macroeconomics of Medium-Term Aid Scaling-Up Scenarios," by Berg and others (2010)—was developed to inform policy discussions at the United Nations on the macroeconomic impact of raising official development assistance (ODA) to low-income countries (LICs) in line with Gleneagles commitments.

The second model—"Public Investment, Growth and Debt Sustainability: Putting Together the Pieces," by Buffie and others (2012)—refines the IMF-World Bank Debt Sustainability Framework (DSF) to account for the public investment, growth, and debt sustainability nexus under alternative financing options. This model is also used in Chapter 3 of the IMF's October 2014 *World Economic Outlook* (IMF 2014a) to simulate the macroeconomic impact of public investment in developing countries more broadly.

The two models mentioned above have many common features—they have similar household types and preferences and, most importantly, both account for key structural characteristics of LICs. They do, however, differ in focus. The first model captures Dutch disease effects that may be brought about by foreign aid inflows, while the second one emphasizes the fiscal reaction of governments to rising public debt stemming from borrowing for public investment financing. Another nice feature of these two models is that they capture key impediments to public investment scaling-up in developing countries, including absorptive capacity constraints. They also assume that only a fraction of each dollar spent in public investment is transformed into capital, owing to investment inefficiency.

The main findings can be summarized as follows: (1) scaling up ODA to Burkina Faso in line with the Gleneagles agreement would have somewhat moderate but long-lasting positive effects on economic growth; these effects would be uneven across sectors, with the nontradables sector benefiting the most and tradables being somewhat affected by the Dutch disease; (2) Burkina Faso would capture a higher growth premium if a large share of the additional foreign aid is allocated to public investment; and (3) the massive investment scaling-up contemplated under the country's updated growth and poverty reduction strategy, while boosting medium- and long-term growth, would jeopardize debt sustainability under plausible assumptions on tax adjustment and concessional financing. A more gradual approach to closing the country's infrastructure gap is, therefore, desirable, because it would allow the country to address its capacity constraints and to improve the efficiency of public investment.

More generally, the two models used in this paper are very useful tools for assessing the macroeconomics of scaling up foreign aid and public investment while preserving debt sustainability, and results obtained herein could be informative for a wide range of developing countries. Nonetheless, the application to Burkina Faso has highlighted a few caveats that should be kept in mind when interpreting simulation results and when extending the related policy recommendations to other countries. For instance, the first model does not account for the composition for ODA between aid and loans, which is critical for public debt sustainability. In addition, tax adjustment in the second model solely takes the form of tax rate adjustments. However, the low tax-to-GDP ratio in many LICs (well below the headline value-added tax rate in most cases) suggests that important revenue gains could be achieved through enhanced revenue administration (for given tax rates), including by broadening the tax base to include, for example, the informal sector. Also, neither of the two models accounts for dynamic improvement in countries' absorptive capacity and (potential) gains in public investment efficiency that may be achieved as countries complete the scaling-up process. We highlight these caveats and a few others in presenting the results throughout the paper.

The remainder of the paper is organized as follows: Section II provides some background on the Burkinabè economy, Section III discusses the scenario in which public investment is financed solely via foreign aid, Section IV discusses public investment financing through a combination of tax adjustment and borrowing, and Section V concludes and draws policy recommendations.

II. Background: Economic and Social Environment

Burkina Faso's economic performance has been generally strong during the past decade (Appendix B, Figure 1), although many impediments to broad-based growth remain. Sustained implementation of sound policies and structural reforms has contributed to a stable macroeconomic environment supportive of private sector development and poverty reduction. Economic growth has been driven mainly by agriculture and services. With the onset of gold production in 2007, the mining sector's contribution to growth has increased but remains modest. Inflation has been moderate, except for spikes driven by exogenous shocks, including terms of trade and natural disasters that affect agriculture production. The external position has strengthened in recent years, reflecting favorable developments in cotton and gold exports; and the financial sector has remained broadly sound.

Despite this progress, deep-seated structural weaknesses continue to hinder economic growth, and the economy remains highly vulnerable to weather-related and terms-of-trade shocks as mentioned above. In addition, despite recent progress under the World Bank *Doing Business* indicators,[4] significant efforts are needed to reduce transaction costs and further improve the business environment. Burkina Faso ranked 135 out of 144 countries in the 2014–15 *Global Competitiveness Report* (Schwab 2014), a slight deterioration from 2012–13 when the country ranked 133. The report identified limited access to financing, corruption, inadequate supply of infrastructure, inefficient government bureaucracy, poor tax regulations, and inadequately educated workforce as some of the key factors hindering private sector development in Burkina Faso.

Revenue collection improved significantly in the past 10 years, with tax revenue rising from 10 percent of GDP in 2000 to 16.7 percent in 2013, thanks to continued administrative efficiency gains and tax reform measures. However, external resources

---

[4] Burkina Faso's ranking improved from 154 under the 2010 *Doing Business* indicators to 151 under the 2011 indicators (out of 183 countries).

still make up a large part of the country's budget, with grants and external loans financing an average of 40 percent of public spending during 2000–10 (excluding debt relief in 2006) and projected to stand at 28 percent in 2014. One medium-term fiscal policy challenge is to sustain fiscal consolidation efforts to reduce the budget's vulnerability, to aid swings and scale up public investment to support private sector–led growth.

Burkina Faso's export base is narrow. Exports are dominated by cotton and gold, making the external position highly vulnerable to fluctuations in global commodity prices and weather conditions that affect cotton production. There is potential for diversification, notably in agriculture, agribusiness, and mining. However, realizing this potential requires sizable public and private investment, a business environment conducive to private sector development, and continued implementation of growth-enhancing policies and reforms. Regarding external debt policy, the debt sustainability analyses show that to preserve medium- to long-term debt sustainability, Burkina Faso should continue to cover financing needs largely with grants and concessional loans. Other sources of investment financing, including nonconcessional borrowing and public-private partnerships, should be used cautiously to contain contingent liabilities or be reserved for high-return projects.

Progress toward the achievement of the Millennium Development Goals (MDGs) was very slow. The country's 2010 MDG status report indicated that only two of the 21 targets were likely to be met, and two were potentially achievable (Appendix B, Figure 2). External and domestic shocks slowed progress toward the MDGs, including the impact of the 2007–08 spikes in global food and fuel prices that diverted household resources away from other priority spending areas such as health and education; weather-related shocks that exacerbate the precarious conditions of vulnerable groups, notably in rural areas; and geopolitical factors, notably the Ivoirien and Malian crises that pulled thousands of refugees into the country. In 2012, Burkina Faso adopted the MDG acceleration framework (MAF)—a targeting tool proposed by the United Nations to bolster progress in lagging areas. Given its vulnerability to climate shocks and the persistence of food insecurity, Burkina Faso decided under the MAF to focus on eradicating extreme poverty and hunger (MDG1), particularly for food security and nutrition.

The Poverty Reduction Strategy Paper (PRSP) for 2011–15, titled SCADD (*Stratégie de Croissance Accélérée et de Développement Durable*),[5] sought to achieve strong and sustained economic growth while strengthening progress toward the MDGs and poverty reduction. Macroeconomic policies and reforms under the SCADD supported economic diversification, enhanced absorptive capacity for public investment, increased investment in infrastructure, and an improved business environment. In particular, the SCADD emphasized increasing public investment to support private sector–led growth and closing the country's infrastructure gap. The implementation of the strategy was estimated to cost about US$15 billion for 2011–15, including a doubling of the public investment budget to reach US$2.2 billion in 2015.[6] Aid scaling-up under the Gleneagles initiative would provide much-needed financing to the authorities' development strategy. We examine below the macroeconomics of this investment scaling-up plan under alternative financing options, including through foreign aid and a combination of tax adjustment and borrowing. We put particular emphasis on public debt sustainability (financing through borrowing) and on Dutch disease effects (financing through foreign aid).

---

[5] Strategy for Accelerated Growth and Sustained Development.

[6] As stated in the SCADD document, the strategy adopts an approach to poverty reduction that is more focused on developing the productive capacities of the Burkinabè economy.

III. Investment Scaling-Up Financed by Aid without Fiscal Adjustment

A. SETTING OF AID SCALING-UP

This section assesses the macroeconomic impact of an aid surge in Burkina Faso, of the magnitude of the Gleneagles commitment, and draws policy recommendations to mitigate potential adverse effects on the economy.

During the 2005 G8 summit, donors pledged to assist African countries in reaching the MDGs through an increase in ODA[7] by US$25 billion a year by 2010, compared with 2004 levels. For Burkina Faso, fulfillment of the Gleneagles commitment would lead to scaling up aid to US$85 per capita per year through an increase in ODA flows by 5.1 percent of GDP to reach 18 percent. In 2009, net ODA flows to Burkina Faso amounted to some US$957 million in constant 2004 U.S. dollar terms. Hence, to meet the Gleneagles commitment, aid flows would have to increase by US$383 million in total (US$24.3 per capita) to US$1.3 billion before end-2015. Although an increase in aid of

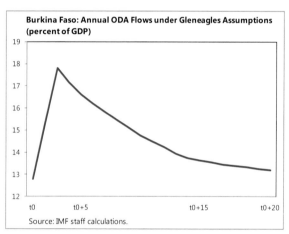

Burkina Faso: Annual ODA Flows under Gleneagles Assumptions (percent of GDP)

Source: IMF staff calculations.

that magnitude may generate a number of benefits for Burkina Faso, it could potentially generate adverse effects on the economy, particularly in the tradables sector (Dutch disease), depending on real exchange rate dynamics.

The aid scaling-up is assumed to take place within two years before aid declines gradually to historical trends. Aid would presumably rise from 12.8 percent of GDP—the level in 2009—at year 0 to about 18 percent in year 2 before decelerating. This

---

[7] ODA is defined as project and program grants and concessional loans with a grant element of 35 percent or more.

assumption is compatible with the authorities' ambition to scale up public investment under the 2011–15 PRSP.

B. MODEL PRESENTATION—BASELINE ASSUMPTIONS AND CALIBRATION

The macroeconomic impact of the aid surge is analyzed using a new Keynesian DGE model developed by Berg and others (2010) calibrated to the Burkinabè economy. The model examines the aggregate and sectoral (tradable and nontradable goods sectors) implications of a surge in foreign aid in LICs. The nontraded goods sector features monopolistic competition, while the traded goods sector is perfectly competitive—traded goods are perfectly mobile across countries and the representative domestic firm in that sector takes international prices as given (Box 1).

To account for the country's economic features, this paper calibrates the above model using data and studies on Burkina Faso, notably its pegged exchange rate regime and the small size of its financial and tradables sectors. The steady state ratios are calibrated on the country's National Accounts, using 2009 as the base year (see Appendix A). In particular, the relative size of the tradable goods sector has important implications for the simulation results. These characteristics are also taken into account in the policy recommendations to mitigate the adverse effects of the shock.

Some other key parameters of the model are calibrated on the basis of existing studies relevant for Burkina Faso. In particular, the extent of financial market imperfection—captured in the model by the proportion of households with access to financial markets—is proxied by the ratio of adults holding a bank account. Surveys suggest that this ratio stands at 16.7 percent in Burkina Faso (see The World Bank

Group, 2010).[8] Also, the demand elasticity for imported goods—which are substitutes for domestically traded goods—is calibrated at 1.15, in line with Tokarick 2010.[9]

The effectiveness of aid inflows to Burkina Faso would depend heavily on the efficiency of public investment and the extent of capacity constraints facing the country. We assume that only 40 percent of investment expenditure actually gets transformed into public capital, in line with Berg and others 2010.[10] The model also accounts for capacity constraints in implementing investment programs by penalizing high-pace public spending. Finally, consistent with similar studies, preference and technology parameters are kept at their level in the reference study by Berg and others (2010) because relevant micro- or macroeconomic evidence is not available for Burkina Faso. However, we perform sensitivity analysis on most of these parameters to ensure the robustness of simulation results.

The composition of expenditure financed with the additional aid is one of the key determinants of the model's quantitative results. First, the allocation of aid between capital and current expenditure highlights the trade-off between the short-term gains of current spending—demand effects—and the long-term gains of capital expenditure—supply effects. The latter, by raising the stock of public capital, increases the marginal productivity of private capital and crowds-in private investment. Broadly in line with the budget, we assume in the baseline scenario that the government allocates half of the additional ODA to capital expenditure and the other half to current spending. Indeed, even though the country's primary goal is to boost investment as much as possible, such increase in capital expenditure must be accompanied with an increase in current expenditures to ensure an appropriate efficiency in using the resulting additional physical capital (for example, operational

---

[8] The 2010 *Financial Access* report estimates that 6.7 percent of adults hold an account in a commercial bank and 10 percent in microfinance institutions. The calibrated value of 16.7 percent is therefore an upper bound, given that some households might hold accounts in both types of financial institutions. However, the calibrated value is realistic if widespread informal financing systems such as rotating savings are taken into account. Sensitivity analysis using values between 6.7 percent and 16.7 percent show minor differences in the results.

[9] The corresponding value in the case of Uganda is 0.79 (see Berg and others 2010).

[10] In the next section, where the scaling-up of public investment is financed mainly through domestic resources, we calibrate the efficiency parameter using the cross-country distribution of the Public Investment Management Index (PIMI).

and maintenance costs). Unfortunately, the model does not distinguish between different types of recurrent spending (for example, those related to human capital vs. others) and as such does not capture the potential complementarities between some specific forms of recurrent spending and physical capital accumulation.

Second, the allocation of aid between traded and nontraded goods determines the level of the additional demand of nontraded goods and, hence, the magnitude of Dutch disease effects on the traded goods sector. In line with national account statistics, we assume that under the baseline scenario, 48 percent of the additional aid is allocated to the nontraded goods sector. We subsequently explore policy options where the government modifies the composition of expenditure financed through the aid surge to increase its beneficial effects and limit its adverse effects on the traded goods sector. We examine in particular a scenario in which the entirety of the aid surge is used to finance public investment, given the ambitious investment plan contemplated by Burkinabè authorities under the country's new growth strategy.

Because Burkina Faso is part of a monetary union with pooled reserves, we assume that the entire amount of aid inflows will be transformed into domestic currency by the regional central bank (the BCEAO)[11] and passed on to the government (full absorption of aid). We also assume that there is no sterilization—sterilization would have little impact on monetary conditions in Burkina Faso, where banks are typically highly liquid.

---

[11] Banque Centrale des Etats de l'Afrique de l'Ouest.

Box 1. Description of the Model Used for Aid Scaling-Up[1]

The framework is a new Keynesian dynamic general equilibrium model for a small open economy. The country produces nontradable and tradable goods. The latter can be exported on international markets and there are imported goods that can be substituted to them.

The economy is populated by four types of agents: households, firms, a government, and a monetary authority. There are two types of households: (1) "savers" who have access to financial markets and smooth consumption by adjusting their holding of cash and domestic and foreign bonds, and (2) financially constrained households ("hand-to-mouth" or "non-savers") that do not have access to financial markets and therefore consume all their current labor income. Two elements are essential in the decision process of households: the composition of their consumption basket in terms of nontradable and tradable goods and the sector to which they supply labor. Household skills are assumed to be somewhat sector-specific, limiting the extent of labor mobility across sectors.

There is a continuum of monopolistically competitive firms in the nontraded goods sector, each of which produces a variety of homogenous nontraded goods. These firms take their demand schedule as given and incur costs in adjusting their prices, in line with Rotemberg 1982. Because firms are identical, the price-setting mechanism results in a consolidated new Keynesian Phillips curve whereby inflation in the nontradables sector depends on the marginal cost of firms and the expected inflation. The representative firm in the tradable goods sector is a price taker and makes zero profits, as tradable goods are assumed to be perfectly mobile. In addition, all firms in the economy are subject to investment adjustment costs—as in Christiano, Eichenbaum, and Evans 2005—which results in a relatively smooth investment path. Technology also features learning-by-doing externalities to capture the Dutch disease that a surge in foreign aid may trigger, on the back of real exchange rate appreciation.

The model also features a government that relies on various sources of financing: foreign aid, labor income taxes, bond issuances on the domestic financial market, and use of its deposits at the central bank. The government allocates part of its revenue to the financing of current operations (transfers to hand-to-mouth consumers and current consumption spending), and devotes another part to building public physical capital—a key feature of the model—albeit with some inefficiencies.

The monetary authority controls the level of reserve money through open-market operations and chooses the appropriate amount of reserves holdings, consistent—for Burkina Faso—with a fixed exchange rate regime.

[1]Details of the model are available at www.imf.org/external/pubs/ft/wp/2010/wp10160.pdf.

C. SIMULATION RESULTS UNDER THE BASELINE SCENARIO

Simulations show that the increase in aid has a positive impact on economic growth (Appendix C, Figure 3). Real GDP growth increases in response to the aid surge by more than 1.4 percentage points in the long term. During the scaling-up episode, the Burkinabè government uses the additional aid to finance higher current and capital expenditure, thus boosting real GDP growth in the short term. The increased government investment accelerates public capital accumulation, triggering other growth-enhancing economic dynamics—notably by increasing the marginal productivity of private capital and the crowding-in of private investment—with longer-lasting effects. After a short period of adjustment, real GDP accelerates for 10 years before decelerating gradually.

The gains in aggregate output come at the cost of higher inflation in the short term and important sectoral disparities. During the scaling-up episode, the government allocates part of the aid proceeds to the purchase of domestic nontradables, generating demand pressure in the nontradables sector. Because price adjustment is costly, firms accommodate the extra demand in the short term mainly by increasing supply. In this process, they increase labor demand in the nontradables sector, driving real wages up, a phenomenon that is exacerbated by capacity constraints. The wage increase in turn triggers two effects: (1) it attracts more labor into the nontradables sector at the expense of the tradables sector, causing the latter to shrink; and (2) it increases the price of the nontraded good (as firms in that sector factor marginal costs into their pricing), which triggers an appreciation of the real exchange rate and a loss in competitiveness. This results in a further decline in the supply of tradables, a self-reinforcing process—the shrinking of the tradables sector erodes its productivity as firms *forget by not doing*, leading to a further decline in production in subsequent years.

The stock of public capital increases as the government allocates part of the additional aid to public investment. The ensuing higher level of public capital stock increases the marginal productivity of private capital, inducing firms to invest more, albeit slowly because of investment-adjustment costs. Eventually, firms in the tradables sector start enjoying learning-by-doing effects as the higher capital stock is supplemented by the reallocation of labor from the nontradables to the tradables sector after the aid scaling-up episode—given that public demand for nontradables decreases to steady state levels. These dynamics trigger the recovery in the tradables sector over the medium term while the nontradables sector continues to expand, although at a slower pace than initially, as aid inflows decelerate gradually.

The impact of the aid surge would be uneven across the tradables and nontradables sectors. The nontradables sector expands significantly and the adverse effects of the aid surge on the tradables sector are somewhat contained, notably because of its relatively small size in Burkina Faso. The tradables sector is estimated to shrink by only about 2 percentage points in the short term, even though the ratio of tradable to nontradable goods' prices is expected to decrease by more than 5 percentage points.[12] However, as growth prospects improve, the sector would recover fully, within six years of the beginning of the aid surge. In the long term, supply in the tradables sector would remain higher than in the steady state period by a little bit more than 1 percentage point. Conversely, growth in the nontradables sector would rise above 3 percentage points before converging to the (lower) growth level in the tradables sector.

D. SENSITIVITY ANALYSES

This section demonstrates the robustness of results obtained under the baseline scenario and shows how results would be altered if the aid scaling-up takes place differently than assumed under the baseline. Sensitivity analyses on a number of steady state parameters show that the simulated impact of the aid scaling-up on the Burkinabè economy remains broadly unchanged when assumptions are slightly different from those adopted under the baseline. In particular, results do not change drastically when we compute the economy's steady state characteristics using the following:

- The average values for 2006–10;
- The post-2009 export-to-GDP ratio, to account for soaring gold exports; and
- Alternative values for households' access to financial assets.

Sensitivity analyses on the schedule and amount of disbursement show that if the aid scaling-up takes longer than two years to materialize or is lower than assumed, the magnitude of the impact on growth would be altered, but not its direction. In most countries, including Burkina Faso's main donors,[13] recovery from the global financial

---

[12] Because Burkina Faso's currency (the CFA franc) is pegged to the euro, the nominal exchange rate remains flat, leading to an even higher real exchange rate appreciation.

[13] The World Bank and the European Union are the main providers of budgetary support to Burkina Faso, with disbursements totaling 66 percent of the country's budget support in 2010. Other main bilateral contributors include Netherlands (8 percent in 2010) and Sweden (about 5.6 percent in 2010).

crisis is still sluggish. Hence, assuming that aid disbursements will be stepped up to levels consistent with the Gleneagles commitment within a period of two years seems overly ambitious. To account for this factor, we first analyze how the results would be altered if the disbursement period is extended from two to five years, keeping other assumptions unchanged (Appendix C, Figure 4).[14] Simulations show that because aid would rise less sharply than under the baseline scenario, ODA-related government spending would increase more progressively in the short term, which would limit the increase in real wages and in the prices of nontradable goods compared with the baseline scenario. Hence, the shift of resources from the tradables to the nontradables sector would be dampened and interest rates would rise only marginally, limiting the crowding-out of private investment. As a result, real GDP growth would be moderate during the scaling-up episode (in the short term) but would prove stronger after three years and more sustainable, with a permanent effect almost 1 percentage point higher than under the baseline scenario. Second, simulations similarly show that if the ODA increase is lower than the Gleneagles-committed level, the impact observed under the baseline scenario would be scaled down proportionally—the magnitude of all the dynamics triggered by the aid surge, both the adverse and the positive economic effects, would be lower. In particular, if ODA does not increase enough, the growth impact could be lower than under the baseline scenario both in the short and long term. The most extreme case is one in which ODA does not increase at all or decreases compared to the steady state.

E. SIMULATION RESULTS UNDER ALTERNATIVE POLICY SCENARIOS

The macroeconomic effects of the aid scaling-up under the baseline scenario are contingent on the authorities' policy choices. The results obtained under the baseline scenario assume that the economy's characteristics at the steady state prevail during and after the aid scaling-up episode. However, to boost growth further, the Burkinabè authorities could implement some measures to ensure the additional aid is used more effectively. We analyze below the impact of several policy options.

---

[14] This scenario would accommodate new initiatives to finance investment in low-income countries including under Financing for Development.

Current versus capital expenditure

The (above) baseline scenario is calibrated to roughly match the allocation of aid proceeds in Burkina Faso in the budget. We now consider a policy option whereby the government allocates a higher share of aid to building public capital. Figure 5 (Appendix C) portrays the dynamics of key macroeconomic indicators when all the aid inflows are used for investment purposes, hence assuming the budget's regular resources will finance the increase in current expenditure that would be needed to operate and maintain the outcomes of scaled-up investment.[15] The assumption of allocating the entirety of the aid surge to public investment is consistent with the authorities' ambitious public investment plan under the country's 2011–15 PRSP, which includes a doubling of the public investment budget to US$2.2 billion over a five-year period, in an attempt to close its infrastructure gap. While the baseline scenario and this alternative scenario result in output gains of similar magnitudes in the short term, the medium- and long-term gains are substantially higher in the latter. For instance, under the alternative scenario, the impact on aggregate output growth reaches a maximum of 3.5 percent after 10 years, compared with less than 2 percent under the baseline scenario. This alternative scenario does not result in a lower output gain in the short term, simply because investment requires both imported tradables and nontradables.

The preferred policy option would therefore be to allocate a higher share of aid proceeds to public investment. The rationale behind this choice is further strengthened by results under the other extreme case in which the additional aid is fully allocated to current expenditure (Appendix C, Figure 5): the country experiences higher GDP growth only during the transition period corresponding to the aid surge; output subsequently returns to its steady state level, with no permanent dividends from the aid scaling-up.

Efficiency of aid-related spending

Ensuring that the scaled-up aid is spent more efficiently increases the positive effects of the aid surge on capital accumulation and, hence, on growth. While the baseline

---

[15] Examples of such outcomes are public units (that is, hospitals, schools, other administrative entities) or other infrastructures (for example, roads, railways, ports).

scenario assumes that aid-related capital spending is as efficient as in the steady state, we assume under this alternative scenario that the authorities would implement measures aimed at improving the efficiency of the aid-related spending, notably by using the additional aid to finance projects with high returns and allowing streamlined administrative procedures for the use of the aid.[16] Simulation results (Appendix C, Figure 6) show that, in this case, while the levels of public and private investment are similar to the ones under the baseline scenario, the resulting capital stock is higher in the medium to long term. As a result, the growth impact of the aid surge is stronger than under the baseline scenario. In addition, real wages increase more than under the baseline scenario, as firms seek to use more labor to operate the additional capital but are constrained by labor market's rigidities. The other effects remain similar to results under the baseline scenario.

F. CAVEATS

Although it captures many salient features of LICs and accounts for policy trade-off facing policymakers in those countries, the DGE model in Berg and others 2010 remains a simplified version of the real economy, as any such model would. Three potential areas of improvement for Burkina Faso and similar developing countries are as follows:

- The model assumes that foreign tradables are perfect substitutes for domestic tradables. This assumption is questionable for Burkina Faso because exports are mostly dominated by two products (gold and cotton), while imports comprise a diverse basket of goods. Accounting for this would limit the crowding-out effect of the domestic tradables sector implied by the model and lead to a larger short-term aggregate output gain from the aid surge. In addition, as the government devotes part of the aid proceeds to building public capital, imports of capital goods would rise more than implied by the current version of the model, which would deteriorate the current account and worsen the external position further. The aggregate production and

---

[16] In this scenario, we assume that 54 percent of the investment financed with the additional aid is transformed into capital (up from 40 percent under the baseline scenario), which corresponds to the efficiency of capital spending in South Asian countries (Pritchett, 2000).

consumption gains would therefore need to be contrasted with the deterioration of the external account.

- Part of the drop in tradable output in the model comes from the introduction of learning-by-doing effects, which tend to be more prominent in countries with a large export-manufacturing sector. However, as noted above, this is not the case in Burkina Faso. Mining industries are typically owned by foreign companies, and fluctuations in the production of cotton—the country's main exported commodity through 2009—are associated more with climatic conditions than learning-by-doing mechanics.

- The model does not account for the composition of ODA (aid versus loans). Because Burkina Faso is at moderate risk of debt distress, it is important that the increase in ODA to the country includes mainly aid and highly concessional loans. This will also preserve the hard-won improvements in debt sustainability—the country's debt outlook improved from high risk of debt distress prior to 2013 to moderate risk. Introducing the composition of ODA in the model would help gauge the debt sustainability implications of the planned aid scaling-up. The next section does so using a model that accounts for the sources of investment financing.

- The model assumes that limited absorptive capacity could dampen the benefits of aid scaling-up by amplifying public spending inefficiencies. However, more donor financing would arguably provide incentives to speed up the reform agenda to alleviate bottlenecks in public investment execution and thus reduce capacity constraints. Accounting for such positive dynamics in absorptive capacity would increase the benefits of aid scaling-up above the current results.

IV. Investment Scaling-Up Financed through Fiscal Adjustment and Borrowing

This section examines the public investment, growth, and debt sustainability nexus in Burkina Faso. It uses an open-economy DGE model developed by Buffie and others (2012) to simulate the macroeconomic implications of investment scaling-up under various financing options (Box 2). A peculiar feature of our analysis is that the public investment scaling-up herein is tailored to the authorities' 2011–15 PRSP, which increases its policy relevance. The section discusses the financing of the contemplated investment plan, including through a tax policy adjustment and borrowing, with particular focus on fiscal sustainability. The discussion takes into account Burkina Faso's membership to a customs and monetary union, which limits the scope for unilateral adjustment in the value-added tax (VAT) rate and the economy's vulnerability to exogenous shocks.

A. KEY FEATURES OF THE MODEL

One of the sharp criticisms about the DSF is that debt projections therein are not derived from an internally consistent macroeconomic framework (see, for example, Eaton 2002 and Hjertholm, 2003).[17] Buffie and others (2012) try to address that shortcoming by examining debt sustainability within the public investment-growth nexus, an internally consistent macroeconomic framework. The authors developed an open-economy DGE model that features a government that invests in infrastructure, albeit with some inefficiencies and capacity constraints. To finance its investment needs, the government complements grants and concessional loans with revenue from domestic consumption tax. The economy features two sectors: a traded goods sector and a nontraded goods sector. Firms in both sectors use the nonrival public infrastructure to complement the sector-specific capital and hire labor from households to carry out their productive operations. Households in the model derive

---

[17] It has been pointed out that the DSF does not systematically incorporate the linkages between public capital accumulation and growth, nor does it account for the potential fiscal reaction of governments to rising public debt.

utility from the consumption of the nontraded goods, and from the foreign and domestic traded goods. We calibrate the model to the Burkinabè economy and first simulate the fiscal adjustment path consistent with long-term debt sustainability, taking as given the path of grants and concessional borrowing as projected under the IMF–supported Extended Credit Facility (ECF). We subsequently consider alternative financing sources.

B. CALIBRATION

Similarly to the first section, the model is calibrated to match salient features of the Burkinabè economy. All steady state ratios are based on National Accounts and fiscal data (see Section III and Appendix A for steady state ratios). Some other parameters are calibrated to the average LIC as in Buffie and others 2012, when relevant information is not available for Burkina Faso. We discuss here only parameters and steady state ratios that are specific to Burkina Faso.[18]

The efficiency of public investment has significant implications on the model's quantitative results. To account for various weaknesses in the investment process, including project selection, we assume that 70 cents out of each dollar spent in public investment increases the stock of productive infrastructure. This parameter's value is slightly above the 60 cents per dollar benchmark assumed in Buffie and others 2012, reflecting Burkina Faso's relatively high score in the Public Investment Management Index (PIMI) developed by Dabla-Norris and others (2011)—the country ranks in the fourth quartile of the PIMI distribution in a sample of 71 developing countries.[19] This value is also higher than the assumed efficiency in the previous section where public investment is financed using foreign aid proceeds—

---

[18] The reader may refer to Buffie and others 2012 for the calibration of preferences and technology parameters. These include the intertemporal elasticity of substitution, the elasticity of substitution in consumption, the labor and capital shares in technology, the depreciation rate of capital, and the learning externalities.

[19] The subcomponents of the PIMI suggest that Burkina Faso does relatively well in project selection, management, and ex post evaluation. However, the country performs somewhat poorly in project appraisal.

arguably there could be more oversight on government spending when financial resources are raised domestically.

Public investment is assumed to yield an annual gross return of 25 percent. This value is in the range of values assumed elsewhere in the literature, including in Buffie and others 2012 (see, for example, Dalgaard and Hansen 2005, and Briceno-Garmendia 2010). It should be noted that the parameter captures the return on actual infrastructure (public investment is stripped of inefficiencies). The return on dollars spent would be lower because of leakages.

Box 2. Description of the Model Used for Scaling Up with Fiscal Adjustment[1]

The framework is an open economy dynamic general equilibrium model. The economy is populated by households, firms, and a government. The government invests in infrastructure, a public good that complements private capital. Public investment is assumed not to be fully efficient, as some spending may be wasted or spent on low-return projects. The government also faces capacity constraints in investing, owing to coordination problems or supply bottlenecks. To finance its investment plans, the government complements grants and concessional loans with revenue from domestic consumption tax (tax adjustment), and may borrow domestically or contract external commercial loans if the implied tax adjustment is not realistic. A peculiar feature of the model is indeed that it embeds a reaction function of the government to rising public debt.

The economy features two sectors: a traded goods sector, for which imported substitutes exist, and a nontraded goods sector. Firms in both sectors use the nonrival public infrastructure to complement the sector-specific capital and labor from households to carry out their productive operations. The model also features sector-specific externalities whereby the stock of capital and the deviation of output from the steady state in any sector affect only the productivity of firms in that sector.

Households in the model derive utility from the consumption of the nontraded goods, and the foreign and domestic traded goods. There are two types of households: (1) "savers" who are subject to labor income tax, are charged user fees for infrastructure services, and invest in private capital and domestic and foreign bonds to smooth consumption; and (2) "non-savers" ("hand-to-mouth" consumers) who have no access to financial markets and therefore consume all their current income from wages, lump-sum transfers from the government, and remittances from abroad.

[1]Details of the model are available at www.imf.org/external/pubs/ft/wp/2012/wp12144.pdf.

C. SIMULATION RESULTS AND POLICY IMPLICATIONS

Simulation results suggest that combining concessional borrowing with immediate and unlimited fiscal adjustment appears compatible with long-term debt sustainability but requires a drastic change in tax policy. This scenario assumes a doubling of the public investment budget to US$2.2 billion over a five-year period, in line with the 2011–15 PRSP. The results indicate that the long-term effects of investment scaling-up are positive and substantial. In particular, economic growth increases significantly, particularly in the medium term, benefiting from higher and (relatively) efficient public investment and increased private sector investment. External debt declines to about 20 percent of GDP in the long term, after an initial increase. In the fiscal area, however, taking as given the projected path of official grants,[20] the adjustment needed to supplement concessional loans to cover the public investment scaling-up leads to an increase in the consumption tax rate by more than 10 percentage points in five years, which reflects also the assumed rising cost of infrastructure (Appendix D, Figure 7). This implies that the VAT rate would rise to almost 30 percent, which is neither feasible nor desirable from the macroeconomic viewpoint.

To circumvent the implausible tax adjustment, the model is simulated under the assumption that the VAT rate remains unchanged for the first five years, then is subsequently raised by about 2 percentage points. Under this scenario, additional concessional borrowing is needed to cover the same level of scaled-up public investment as in the baseline scenario.[21] Simulation results point to a positive macroeconomic impact similar to the baseline scenario, with less pronounced negative impact in consumption in the initial years, given that the tax rate does not rise immediately. However, the additional borrowing raises external public debt to almost 60 percent of GDP in the medium term (Appendix D, Figure 8). Although the debt-to-GDP ratio declines subsequently, it remains elevated and raises concerns in terms of capacity to repay, in view of Burkina Faso's narrow tax base.

A staggered VAT rate increase lessens the impact of the fiscal adjustment on real macroeconomic aggregates (compare with the baseline), but deteriorates the long-

---

[20] Based on the macroeconomic framework under the IMF-supported program. The share of project grants in GDP is set at 2.5 percent, its average value over the second half of the 2000s—we focus on project grants because the simulations do not include a scaling-up of current expenditure for which the government may also receive program grants. Remittances account for a tiny share of GDP in Burkina Faso (about 0.2 percent of GDP), perhaps on account of the global financial crisis and informal transfer channels, which are not necessarily captured in official statistics. These (calibrated) GDP shares of grants and remittances are lower than in Buffie and others 2012 (3.5 and 5 percent, respectively).

[21] We assume that concessional loans accrue a nominal interest rate of 2 percent and have an average maturity of 30 years (the time frame of simulations), including a six-year grace period. This implies a grant element of 42.3 percent, which is below the 61 percent value in Buffie and others 2012. Concessional loans in the joint IMF-World Bank debt sustainability analysis for Burkina Faso embed a grant element of 56.8 percent (1.1 percent interest rate; average maturity of 37 years; and a seven-year grace period). Our somewhat conservative assumption on financing terms reflects the fact that the currently (high) grant element is partly driven by the World Bank's financing (64.6 percent grant element against the 56.8 percent average) while Burkina Faso would probably have to rely on non–World Bank financing to scale up concessional financing.

term debt profile. A staggered increase in the VAT rate indeed allows for a smoother fiscal adjustment in the medium term. However, if the scaled-up investment is financed with the additional revenue, and borrowing on commercial terms, the stock of external public debt rises to unsustainable levels in the medium to long term, reaching some 80 percent of GDP after a 30-year period (up from less than 20 percent of GDP at the beginning of the simulation period). Such a buildup of external debt may hamper long-term growth prospects. Accessing non-concessional borrowing to complement concessional financing of scaled-up investment under the PRSP therefore seems incompatible with long-term debt sustainability (Appendix D, Figure 9), given the relatively high cost of commercial borrowing, compared with concessional financing—commercial loans are assumed to accrue a nominal interest rate of 9.9 percent, based on available estimates for Burkina Faso in Gueye and Sy 2010. Imposing a 20 percent cap on the VAT to smooth the fiscal adjustment, simulation results show that, compared with the baseline scenario, the stock of commercial debt increases by almost 10 percentage points of GDP after five years and the total stock of public debt rises above 50 percent of GDP before returning to historical levels. The impact on growth is, however, similar to the baseline scenario, while access to commercial borrowing increases external debt obligations, which may prove challenging considering the country's vulnerability to terms-of-trade shocks.

Simulation results with the public investment path under the ECF-supported program suggest that, while the long-term impact of growth is somewhat lower than in scenarios based on the investment scaling-up under the PRSP, the additional concessional borrowing is compatible with long-term debt sustainability. However, the required fiscal adjustment remains strong, although less drastic than in the baseline scenario.[22] Simulation results show also that a staggered increase in the VAT rate could correct for this effect and provide a smoother fiscal adjustment path. Hence, financing modest increases in public investment through additional revenue—under a staggered tax structure—and concessional borrowing would help avoid undesirable tax hikes and support long-term debt sustainability (Appendix D, Figure 10). Simulation results also suggest that doubling the user fees for

---

[22] The Burkinabè authorities are committed to enhancing tax administration under the ECF program, not modeled here. Accounting for such revenue sources in the model would limit the extent of tax rate adjustment to finance the public investment path under the ECF program.

infrastructure services from the current 40 percent in Burkina Faso[23] would reduce the fiscal adjustment needed to safeguard debt sustainability by about a percentage point.

D. CAVEATS

The model in Buffie and others 2012 is an interesting tool for assessing the impact of scaled-up public investment on growth and on the implications of financing options on long-term debt and fiscal sustainability. Simulation results can be used to inform policy decisions, particularly on: (1) the speed and magnitude of scaled-up investment; (2) implications for financing options and; (3) the required fiscal adjustment. It is worth noting that tax adjustment in the model solely takes the form of a change in the tax rate. However, the relatively low tax-to-GDP ratio in Burkina Faso (about 17 percent) suggests that important revenue gains could be achieved through enhanced revenue administration (for given tax rates). This requires, for example, strengthened tax compliance and measures to lift some informal activities inside the perimeter of the tax system. Such measures, if effective, would limit the reliance on tax rate adjustments.

As is the case with any such exercise, simulation results presented here depend on a number of assumptions. In particular, the model does not incorporate dynamic changes in absorptive capacity whereby the government could scale up public investment at an increasing pace as bottlenecks are removed along the way. Nevertheless, the main policy conclusions appear quite robust to reasonable changes in parameter values.

---

[23] This number is computed as the ratio between the user fees on existing highways in 2010 and their maintenance costs (the raw data were obtained from the Burkinabè authorities).

V. Conclusion and Policy Recommendations

An effective implementation of Burkina Faso's new PRSP would contribute to significant progress in addressing the country's large infrastructure gap, thus enhancing growth prospects and poverty reduction efforts. However, financing constraints are large, and in this paper, we have shown that addressing them would require (1) important revenue mobilization efforts, (2) increased aid, and (3) continued prudent borrowing policies.

Aid scaling-up

Simulation results show that the overall impact of scaling up aid to Burkina Faso is positive: economic growth would increase in the medium term, while inflation would inch up in the short term and return to moderate levels in the years that follow. Sectoral analysis, however, points to short-term disparities between the tradable and nontradable goods sectors, with the former being adversely affected by Dutch disease. Nonetheless, increased investment financed with the additional aid flow would crowd-in private investment, thus leading to permanently higher aggregate output in the medium and long term.

Simulation results also suggest that expenditure composition as well as the time frame for aid scaling-up play an important role. The most efficient spending options are the following: (1) allocating most of the aid increase to public investment and (2) allocating the increased aid to highly efficient investment projects. However, regardless of the spending strategy, the magnitude and the growth effects depend on the disbursement schedule of the aid scaling-up as well.

Implementing measures aimed at removing impediments to growth, especially in the nontradables sector, would also help maximize the growth effects of scaling up aid. Bottlenecks in the nontradables sector limit the positive spillovers of the aid surge on the sector owing to the supply inelasticity, which exacerbates the crowding-out of the tradables sector. Hence, measures aimed at increasing the elasticity of the nontradables supply could increase the benefits associated with the aid surge. In particular, measures to improve the ease of doing business by simplifying procedures for creating enterprises, rationalizing and simplifying the tax system, and improving efficiency and quality in the public administration's service delivery would increase potential gains from scaling up aid. The model suggests that the tradables sector would be crowded out partly because of the loss of competitiveness. Improving the business climate and diversifying production in the tradables sector could thus help dampen Dutch disease effects. Diversification toward goods for which Burkina Faso bears strong comparative advantages would also help shield the tradables sector from the first-round adverse impact of aid scaling-up.

Policies should account for the expected reduction in aid at the end of the scaling-up period. Because aid is expected to decline to levels consistent with past trends at the end of the scaling-up episode, it would be essential for the country to prepare an exit strategy to anticipate on the disruptive impact of the decline in aid and preserve the long-term effects of aid scaling-up on growth. Strengthening revenue mobilization through tax policy and administrative reforms to ensure that stronger revenue collection compensates for the decline in aid during the exit period, and enhancing the business environment while stimulating private sources of financing, is critical in this regard.

The results of the macro-simulations presented in the paper remain valid in the general case of an increase in foreign capital inflows. An increase in aid flows represents an increase in capital inflows because aid is disbursed in foreign currency. Hence, the macroeconomic effects of such shocks are to some extent similar to those of a rise in capital inflows triggered by increasing export receipts, remittances, or royalties. This analysis can therefore serve as a basis for designing appropriate policy responses to other capital inflows–related shocks. Increased windfall from royalties is particularly relevant for Burkina Faso because of the expected expansion in the mining sector over the medium term.

Investment scaling-up with fiscal adjustment and borrowing

Despite a strong long-term macroeconomic impact, scaling up public investment may have adverse implications for debt sustainability or require a drastic short-term fiscal adjustment. Results from a DGE model show that, under certain conditions, scaling up investment to levels envisioned in the authorities' 2011–15 PRSP would raise economic growth substantially in the medium to long term, boost private investment, and increase consumption. The results also highlight that the choice of financing options for the scaled-up investment should be guided by their implications for long-term debt sustainability and the resultant fiscal adjustment.

In particular, simulation results suggest that scaling up public investment with insufficient fiscal adjustment may lead to unsustainable levels of external public debt, which may crowd out private sector investment and hamper long-term growth prospects. Similarly, a drastic fiscal adjustment to finance higher investment may have undesirable macroeconomic effects. Taking into account Burkina Faso's particular circumstances, the results indicate that a better macroeconomic outcome would be achieved if the investment scaling-up is moderate and gradual, and financed with higher grants and concessional loans as well as increased government revenue. The latter could be achieved through a staggered increase in the VAT rate and enhanced collection of user fees on infrastructure services. Enhanced revenue administration—not modeled explicitly here—could lower the extent of tax rate increase implied by the simulations.

A. TABLE: SELECTED STEADY STATE RATIOS

Variables	Calibrated Values
Private consumption	81.8
Of which: Tradables	41.8
Nontradables	40.0
Private investment	8.6
Of which: Tradables	4.6
Nontradables	4.0
Government spending	20.3
Of which: Consumption	12.1
Investment	8.1
Government spending on tradables	10.5
Government spending on nontradables	9.7
Trade balance	-10.7
Exports	12.6
Imports	-23.3
Value added in nontradable sector	53.7
Value added in tradable sector	46.3
Real money balances	12.6
Net foreign asset of the private sector	4.5
International reserves	14.3
Government deposits at the central bank	3.5
Government debt held by the central bank	1.8
Government debt held by the private sector	1.8
Total government debt	3.6
Annualized inflation rate	2.0
Trend growth rate	6.0
Aid	12.8

Sources: Burkinabè authorities and IMF staff estimates.

[1] All values are in percent of GDP, except inflation and the trend growth rate, which are in percent. We estimate the share of tradable goods in total private consumption using the latest National Accounts data (2009) and apply that share to public consumption figures to pin down the consumption of tradable and nontradable goods by the government and households in subsequent years. The share of tradable goods in investment expenditure is estimated using the ratio of capital goods and intermediate goods in total investment. This ratio is estimated separately for private and public investment. The parameters are calibrated using 2009 as the base year (initial steady state).

B. ECONOMIC AND SOCIAL ENVIRONMENT

(a) Figure 1. Selected Economic Indicators, 2000–14

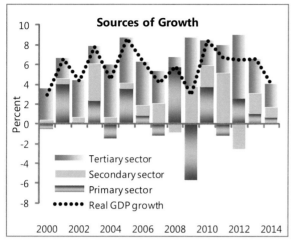

Sources of Growth

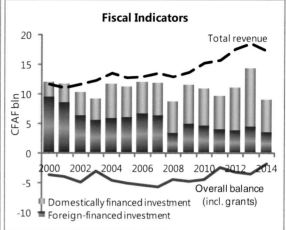

Fiscal Indicators

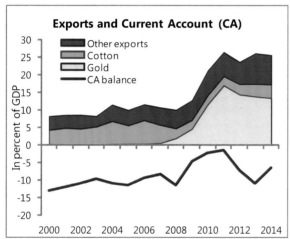

Exports and Current Account (CA)

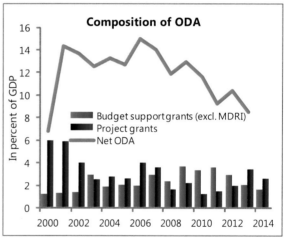

Composition of ODA

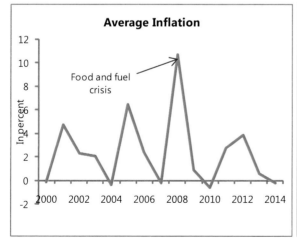

Average Inflation

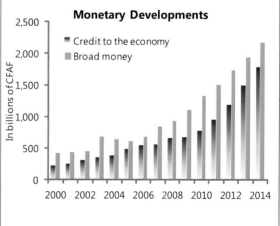

Monetary Developments

Sources: Burkinabè authorities and IMF staff estimates.

(b) Figure 2. Progress toward Millennium Development Goals[1]

Goal 1: Eradicate Extreme Poverty and Hunger

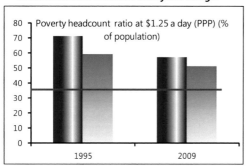

Goal 2: Achieve Universal Primary Education

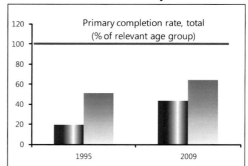

Goal 3: Promote Gender Equality and Empower Women

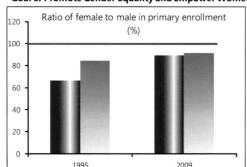

Goal 4: Reduce Child Mortality

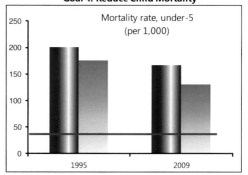

Goal 5: Improve Maternal Health

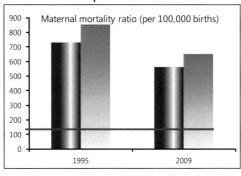

Goal 6: Combat HIV/AIDS, Malaria, and Other Diseases

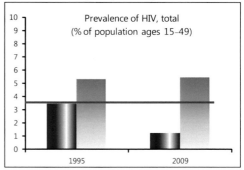

Goal 7: Ensure Environmental Sustainability

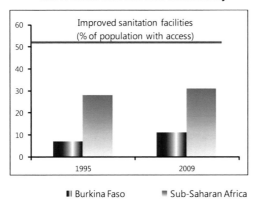

Goal 8: Develop a Global Partnership for Development

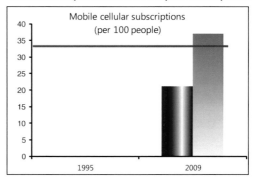

Burkina Faso   Sub-Saharan Africa   ——— 2015 Target for Burkina Faso

Source: World Development Indicators database.

1/ When data were not available for the specific year, the charts use the data from the closest available year.

C. AID SCALING-UP

(c) Figure 3. Baseline Scenario of Aid Scaling-Up

(continued)

Figure 3. Baseline Scenario of Aid Scaling-Up (concluded)

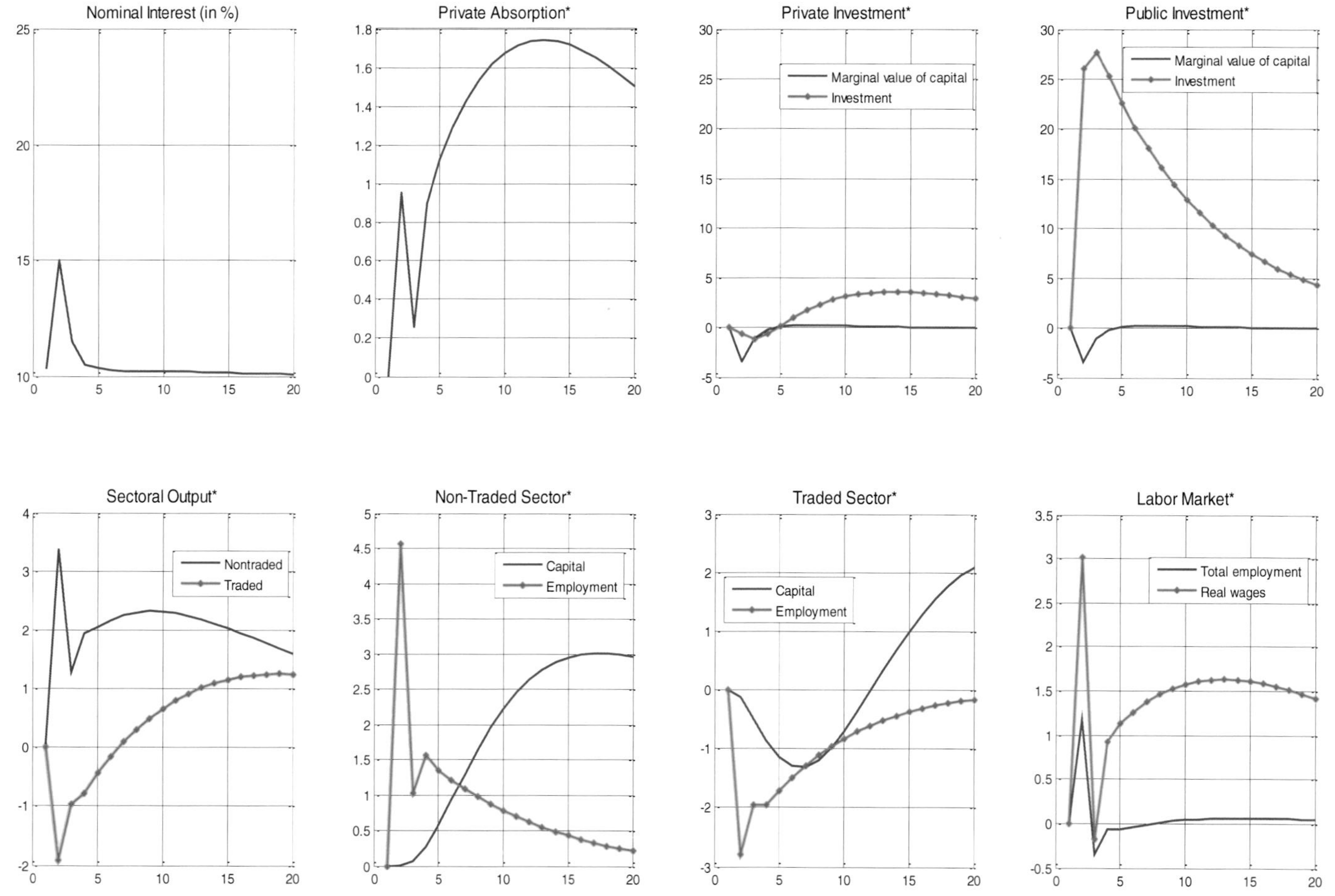

Source: IMF staff calculations.

*Values represent the deviation from the steady state.

(d) Figure 4. Risks to the Baseline Scenario: Aid Scaling-Up Spread over Five Years

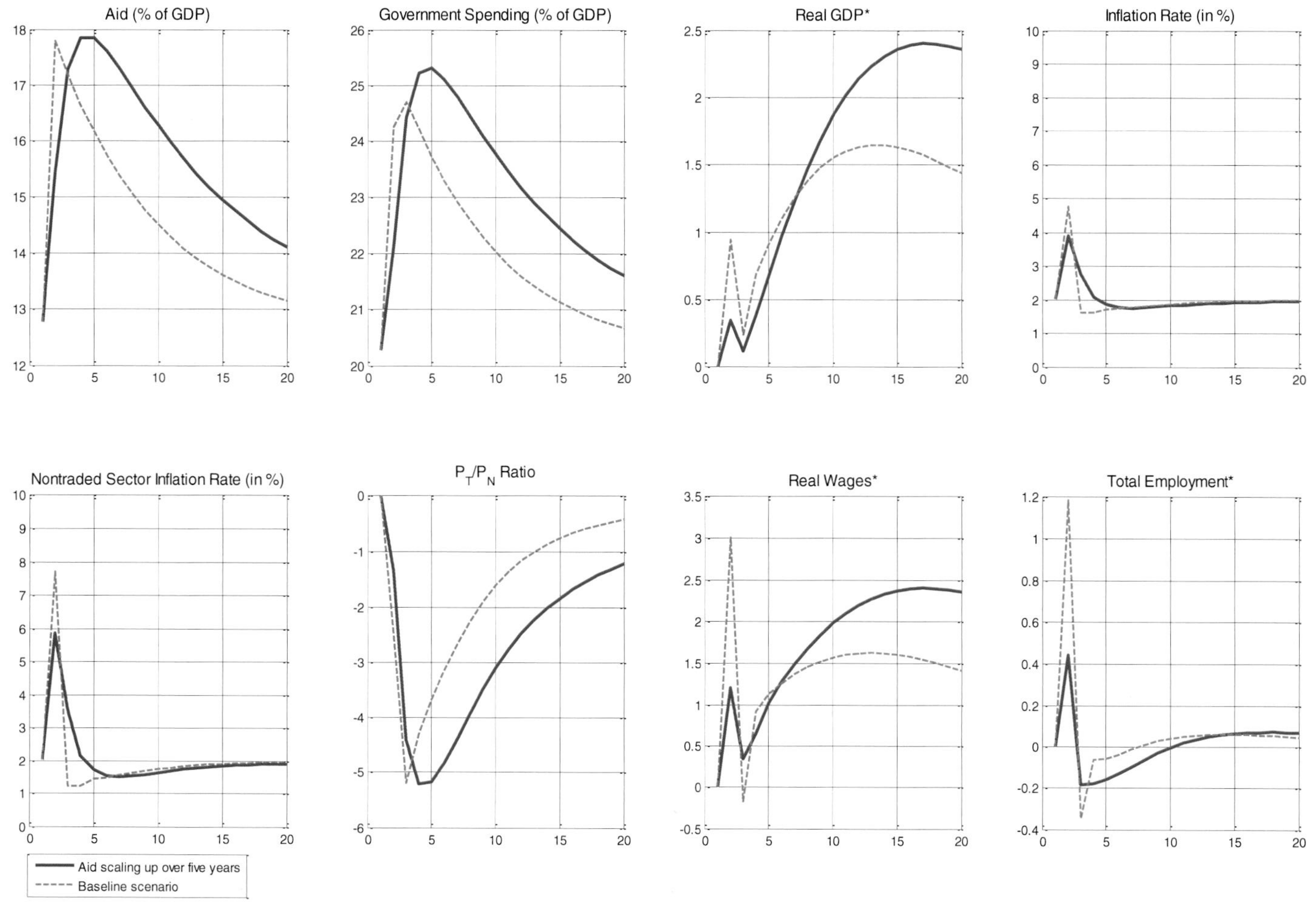

Aid (% of GDP)

Government Spending (% of GDP)

Real GDP*

Inflation Rate (in %)

Nontraded Sector Inflation Rate (in %)

P_T/P_N Ratio

Real Wages*

Total Employment*

Aid scaling up over five years

Baseline scenario

(continued)

Figure 4. Risks to the Baseline Scenario: Aid Scaling-Up Spread over Five Years
(concluded)

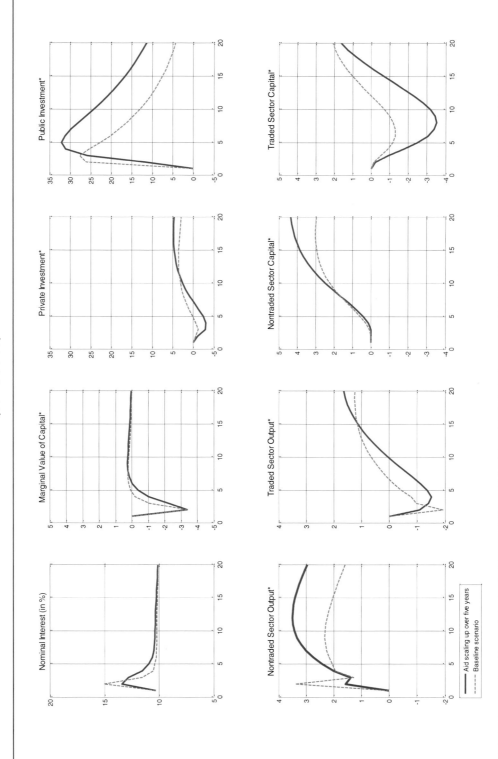

Source: IMF staff calculations.

*Values represent the deviation from the steady state.

(e) Figure 5. Alternative Scenarios A and B: Full Allocation of Aid to Capital Expenditure vs. Full Allocation to Current Expenditure

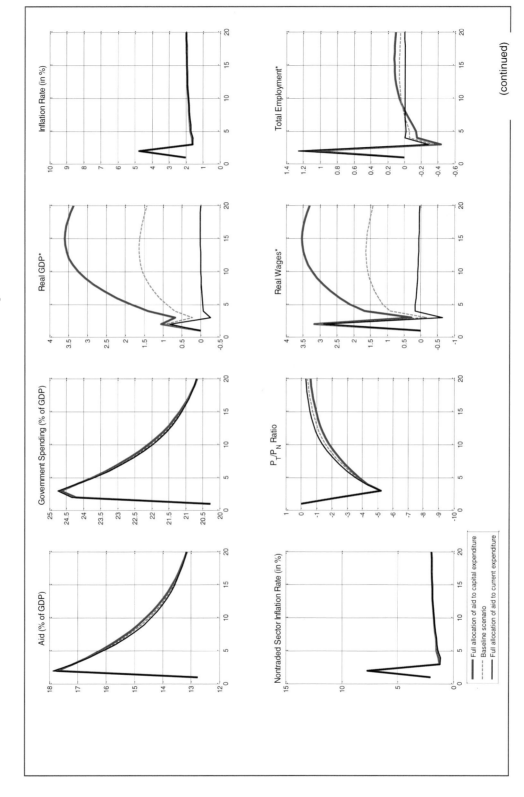

(continued)

Figure 5. Alternative Scenarios A and B: Full Allocation of Aid to Capital Expenditure vs. Full Allocation to Current Expenditure

(concluded)

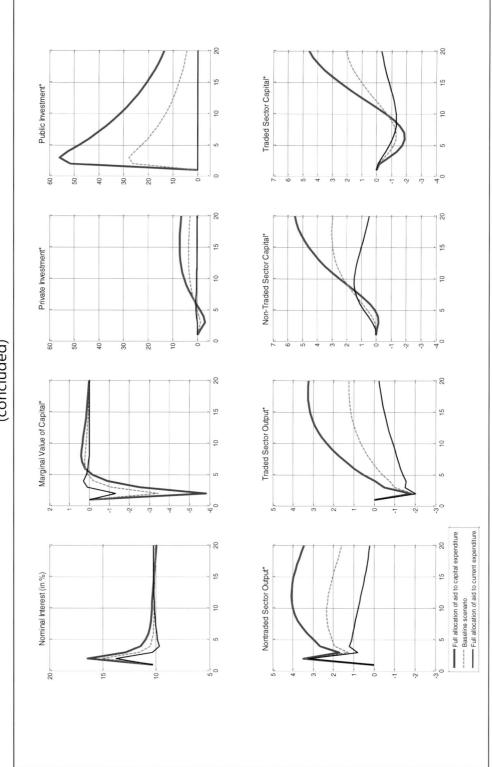

Source: IMF staff calculations.

*Values represent the deviation from the steady state.

(f) Figure 6. Alternative Scenario C: Increased Efficiency of Aid-Related Spending

Aid (% of GDP)

Government Spending (% of GDP)

Real GDP*

Inflation Rate (in %)

Nontraded Sector Inflation Rate (in %)

P_T/P_N Ratio

Real Wages*

Total Employment*

Higher efficiency of aid-related spending
Baseline scenario

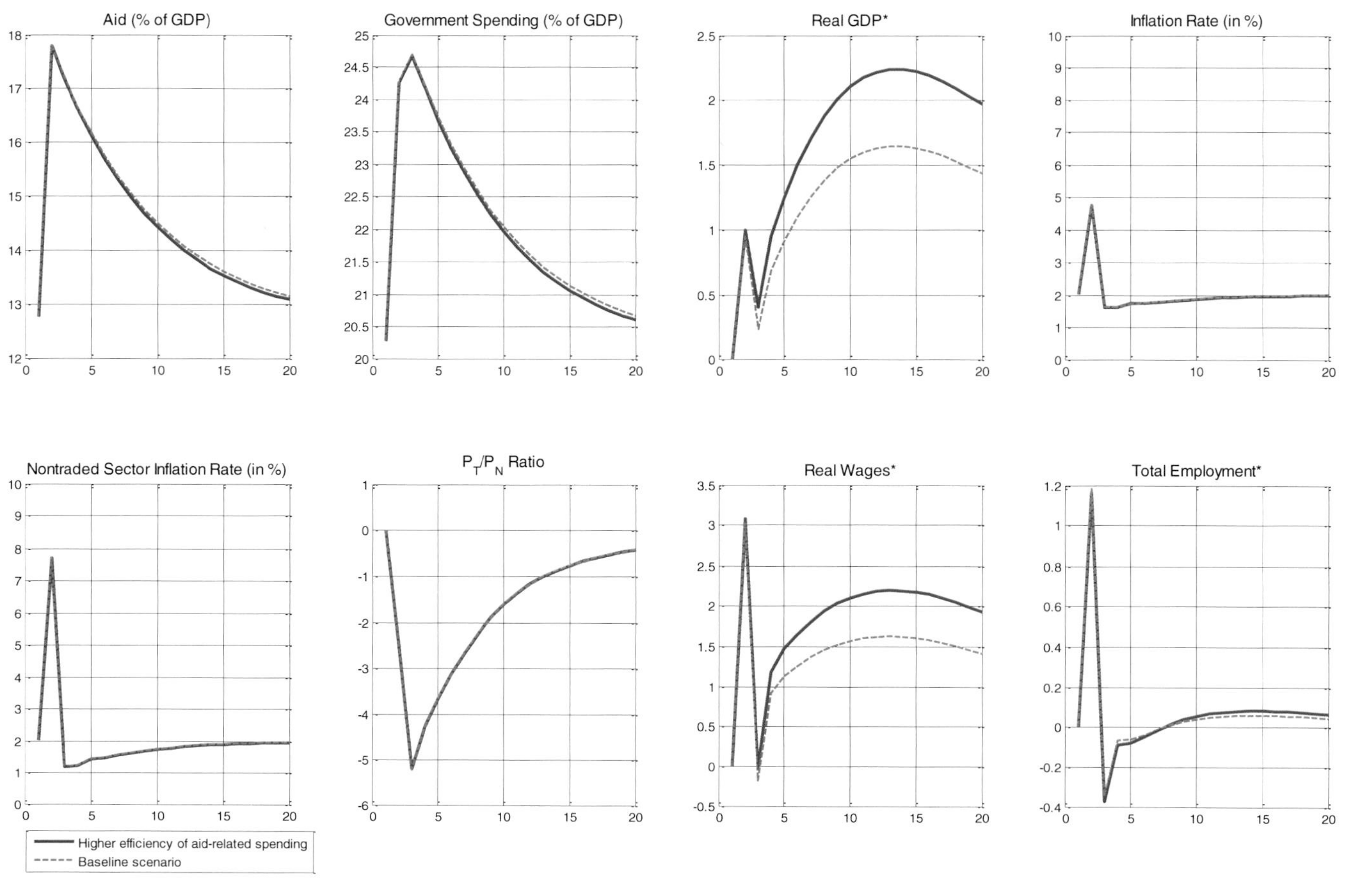

(continued)

Figure 6. Alternative Scenario C: Increased Efficiency of Aid-Related Spending
(concluded)

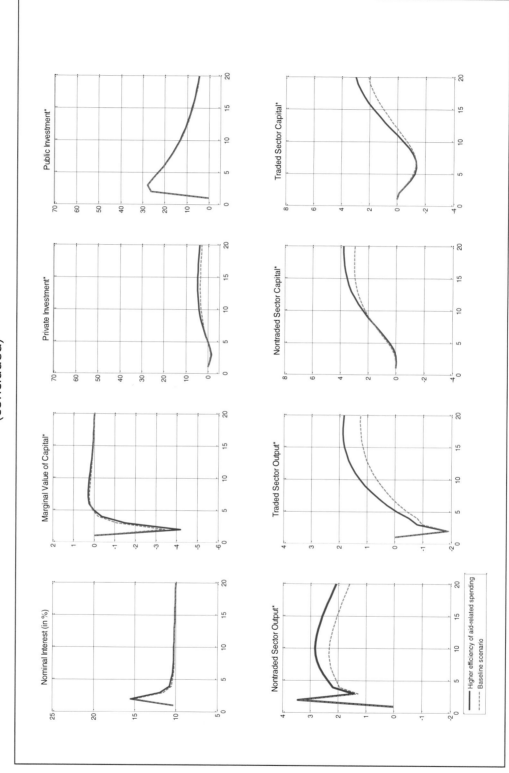

Source: IMF staff calculations.

*Values represent the deviation from the steady state.

D. SCALING UP PUBLIC INVESTMENT THROUGH TAX ADJUSTMENT AND BORROWING

(g) Figure 7. Investment Scaling-Up Financed with Concessional Loans and Unlimited Fiscal Adjustment

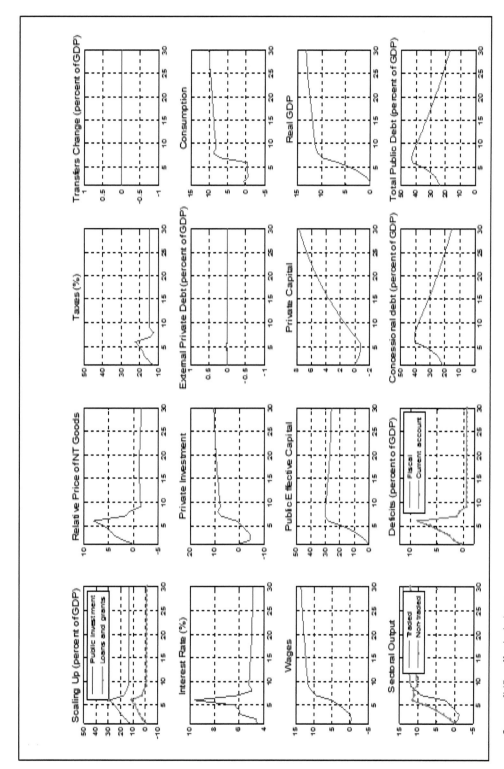

Source: IMF staff calculations.

(h) Figure 8. Investment Scaling-Up Financed with Higher Concessional Loans and Limited Fiscal Adjustment

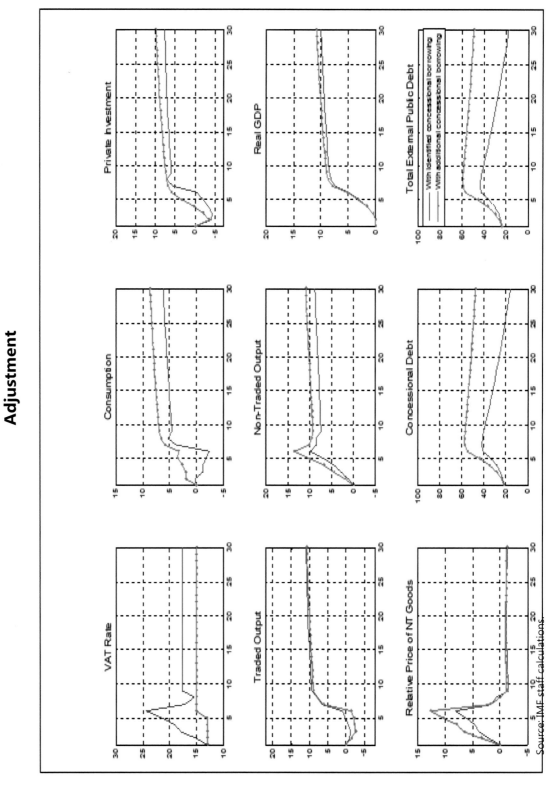

Source: IMF staff calculations.

(i) Figure 9. Investment Scaling-Up: Concessional Borrowing Is Complemented with Commercial Loans and Limited Fiscal Adjustment

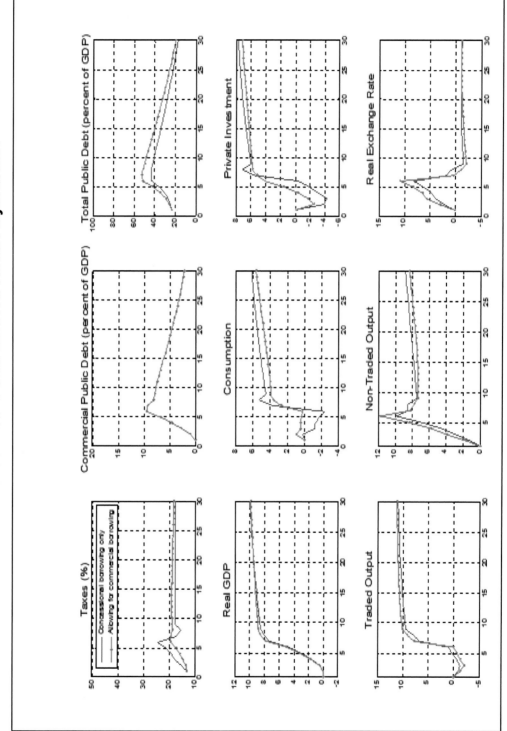

Source: IMF staff calculations.

(j) Figure 10. Moderate Investment Scaling-Up with Concessional Borrowing and a Staggered Tax Adjustment

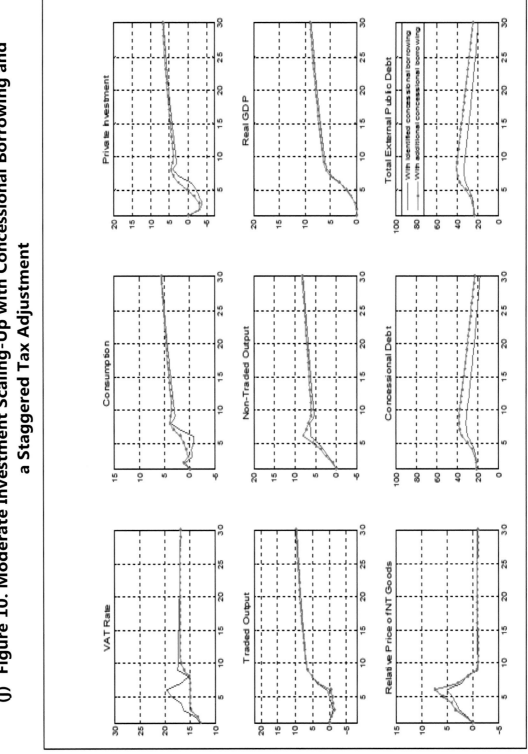

Source: IMF staff calculations.

References

Berg, A., J. Gottschalk, R. Portillo, and F. Zanna. 2010. "The Macroeconomics of Medium-Term Aid Scaling-Up Scenarios." Working Paper 10/160, International Monetary Fund, Washington.

Briceño-Garmendia, C., K. Smits, and V. Foster. 2008. "Financing Public Infrastructure in Sub-Saharan Africa: Patterns and Emerging Issues." AICD Background Paper 15, World Bank, Washington.

Briceño-Garmendia, C., and C. Domínguez-Torres. 2011. "Burkina Faso's Infrastructure: A Continental Perspective", Policy Research Working Paper 5818, World Bank, Washington.

Buffie, E., A. Berg, C. Patillo, R. Portillo, and L. F. Zanna. 2012. "Public Investment, Growth and Debt Sustainability: Putting Together the Pieces." Working Paper 12/144, International Monetary Fund, Washington.

Christiano, L., M. Eichenbaum, and C. Evans. 2005. "Nominal Rigidities and the Dynamic Effects of a Shock to Monetary Policy." *Journal of Political Economy* 113(1): 1–45.

Dabla-Norris, E., J. Brumby, A. Kyobe, Z. Mills, and C. Papageorgiou. 2011. "Investing in Public Investment: An Index of Public Investment Efficiency." Working Paper 11/37, International Monetary Fund, Washington.

Dalgaard, C-J., and W. Hansen. 2005. "Capital utilization and the foundations of club convergence." *Economics Letters*, 87, 145–152.

Diouf, A., and C. Lonkeng Ngouana. 2011. "The Macroeconomics of Scaling-Up Aid: The Case of Burkina Faso." Unpublished, International Monetary Fund.

Eaton, J. 2002. "The HIPC Initiative: The Goals, Additionality, Eligibility, and Debt Sustainability." *Mimeo*, World Bank, Washington.

Eaton 2002 and Hjertholm, 2003

Farah, A., E. Sacerdoti, and G. Salinas. 2009. "The Macroeconomics of Scaling Up Aid: The Case of Niger." Working Paper 09/36, International Monetary Fund, Washington.

Gueye, C., and A. Sy. 2010. "Beyond Aid: How Much Should African Countries Pay to Borrow?" Working Paper 10/140, International Monetary Fund, Washington.

Gupta, S., R. Powell, and Y. Yang. 2006. "Macroeconomic Challenges of Scaling Up Aid to Africa: A Checklist for Practitioners." International Monetary Fund, Washington.

Hjertholm, P. 2003. "Theoretical and Empirical Foundations of HIPC Debt Sustainability Targets." *Journal of Development Studies*, 39, 67–100.

International Monetary Fund (IMF). 2015a. "Fiscal Policy and Long-Term Growth." Washington.

———. 2015b. "Making Public Investment More Efficient." Washington.

———. 2014a. "Is It Time for an Infrastructure Push? The Macroeconomic Effects on Public Investment." Chapter 3 in the *World Economic Outlook*. Washington.

———. 2014b. "Staff Report for the 2014 Article IV Consultation, First Review under the Three-Year Arrangement under the Extended Credit Facility, and Request for Waiver and Modification of Performance Criteria." Country Report No. 14/215, Washington, July.

———. 2013. "Sub-Saharan Africa Regional Economic Outlook." International Monetary Fund, Washington, October.

———. 2012. "Public Investment Scaling-Up, Growth and Debt Sustainability in Burkina Faso." Appendix III in Country Report No. 12/158, Washington, June.

———. 2011. "Linking Public Investment, Growth and Debt Sustainability in Togo." Appendix III in Country Report No. 11/240, Washington, August.

———. 2010. "The Macroeconomics of Scaling-Up Aid: The Case of Zambia." Washington.

———. 2009. "The Macroeconomics of Scaling-Up Aid Scenarios: The Cases of Ghana and Liberia." Washington.

———. 2008a. "The Macroeconomics of Scaling-Up Aid: The Cases of Benin, Niger, and Togo." Washington.

———. 2008b. "The Macroeconomics of Scaling-Up Aid Scenarios: The Cases of the Central African Republic, Rwanda, and Sierra Leone." SM/08/333, Washington.

————. 2005. "The Macroeconomics of Managing Increased Aid Inflows: Experiences of Low-Income Countries and Policy Implications." SM/05/306, Washington.

Ministère de l'Economie et des Finances, and Système des Nations Unies, Burkina Faso. 2010. "Rapport Pays de Suivi des Objectifs du Millénaire pour le développement, Burkina Faso."

Mongardini, J., and I. Samake. 2009. "The Macroeconomics of Scaling Up Aid: The Gleneagles Initiative for Benin." Working Paper 09/115, International Monetary Fund, Washington.

Pritchett, L. 2000. "The Tyranny of Concepts: CUDIE (Cumulated, Depreciated, Investment Effort) Is Not Capital." *Journal of Economic Growth*, Springer, vol. 5(4), pp. 361-84.

Rotemberg, J. 1982. "Sticky Prices in the United States." *Journal of Political Economy* 90: 1187–211.

Schwab, K. 2014. *The Global Competitiveness Report 2014–2015*. World Economic Forum, Geneva.

The World Bank Group. 2010. "Financial Access: The State of Financial Inclusion through the Crisis." The Consultative Group to Assist the Poor (CGAP), Washington.

Tokarick, S. 2010. "A Method for Calculating Export Supply and Import Demand Elasticities." Working Paper 10/180, International Monetary Fund Washington.